SHOW ME THAT I'M EVERYWHERE
AND GET ME HOME FOR TEA.

GEORGE HARRISON

Printed in China

Thanks to Ann Butterworth

Publisher's Cataloging-in-Publication Data:

Usova, Victoria.
  Teapots and assorted things / art by Victoria
Usova ; text by Warren Ross.
    pages cm
  ISBN: 978-0-9903086-0-7 (hardcover)
    1. Watercolor painting. 2. Wit and humor.
3. Picture books.   I. Ross, Warren, 1953- II.
Title.
PS439 .U86 2015
817—dc23

for the Happy Hopper Classroom!
Best wishes,
Warren Ross

TEAPOTS
AND
ASSORTED THINGS

ART BY VICTORIA USOVA

TEXT BY WARREN ROSS

This is me in here.
Is that you out there?

Tea party!
Everyone is coming.

The kite stares at the sky,
looking for new friends.

Here comes Bird Face.
He drinks all kinds of teas.
He feeds his birds with peas.
He built his house from cheese.

Who lives on the first floor?
Pearlabelle Platz.
Who lives on the second floor?
Dogs and cats.
Who lives on the third floor?
Boogaloo Spats.
Who lives on the fourth floor?
Bugs and bats.
Who lives on the fifth floor?
Ducks with hats.
Who lives up in the attic?
The baker who rides the bike.

Anna was so nervous
about her new hat,
she forgot to pour tea
for the mice.

He told me he was the Moon.
But I knew he was really
the Runaway Pancake.
"I'll keep your secret," I said.

I'm off.
Up, up, up
to Bird School
to learn with the birds.

Tonight we had the first meeting
of our Standing in the Snow Club.

It's my birthday.
I'll walk around the world.

Under the snow cherries,
under the snow,
we have a place to go,
for tea.

All the things I ever thought
are air mail in the air,
flying everywhere.